Little Pebble™

MIGHTY MILITARY MACHINES

Drones

A 4D BOOK

by Matt Scheff

PEBBLE
a capstone imprint

This is a Capstone 4D book!

Want fun videos that go with this book?

Just visit www.capstone4d.com

Use this password
drones.01143

Little Pebble is published by Pebble
1710 Roe Crest Drive, North Mankato, Minnesota 56003
www.capstonepub.com

Library of Congress Cataloging-in-Publication data is available from the Library of Congress website.
ISBN 978-1-9771-0114-3 (hardcover)
ISBN 978-1-9771-0120-4 (paperback)
ISBN 978-1-9771-0126-6 (eBook PDF)

Editorial Credits
Marissa Kirkman, editor; Heidi Thompson, designer;
Jo Miller, media researcher; Tori Abraham, production specialist

Photo Credits
Air National Guard photo by Senior Airman Michael Quiboloy, 9, Tech. Sgt. Neil Ballecer, 19;
U.S. Air Force photo by Airman 1st Class Aaron Montoya, 12, 17, Master Sgt. Robert W. Valenca, 5, Master Sgt. Steve Horton, 13, Tech Sgt. Effrain Lopez, cover, Tech. Sgt. Kevin J. Gruenwald, 11;
Visual Information Specialist Paolo Bovo, 7; U.S. Navy: Photo courtesy of Northrop Grumman, 15; Wikimedia: U.S. Air Force photo, 21
Design Elements: Shutterstock: Zerbor

Printed in the United States   5062

Table of Contents

Drones

Zoom!

What is in the sky?

It is a drone.

Drones fly.

Some are large.

Others are small.

Take Off

A drone takes off.

It is fast.

Pilots fly drones.

They sit in a control room.

Parts

Drones can spy.

They take pictures.

camera

13

Boom! Pow!

Some drones can shoot.

This is the engine.

It powers the drone.

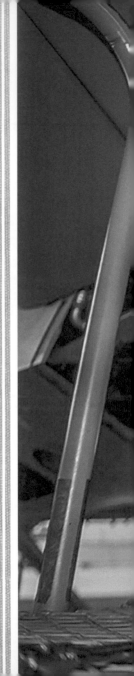

engine

The wings lift the drone.

It flies high and far.

wings

Look up!

There goes a drone!

Glossary

control room—a room with equipment used to command machines that is a distance away from the machines

engine—a machine that makes the power needed to move something

pilot—the person who flies a jet or plane

spy—to collect information about an enemy in secret

wings—the parts of a plane that stick out on each side of the aircraft that make it able to fly

Read More

Doeden, Matt. *The U.S. Air Force.* The U.S. Military Branches. North Mankato, Minn.: Capstone Press, 2018.

Parkes, Elle. *Hooray for Pilots!* Hooray for Community Helpers! Minneapolis: Lerner Publications, 2016.

Von Finn, Denny. *Predator Drones.* Epic Books: Military Vehicles. Minneapolis: Bellwether Media, 2013.

Internet Sites

Use FactHound to find Internet sites related to this book.

Visit *www.facthound.com*
Just type in 9781977101143 and go.

Super-cool stuff! Check out projects, games and lots more at **www.capstonekids.com**

Critical Thinking Questions

1. Who flies a drone?

2. What do drones do when they are spying?

3. Which part gives a drone its power?

Index